First published in Great Britain in 2003
by Zero To Ten Limited,
part of the Evans Publishing Group,
2A Portman Mansions, Chiltern St, London W1U 6NR

British Library Cataloguing in Publication Data
Clibbon, Meg
Imagine you're a knight!
1. Knights and knighthood – Juvenile literature
I. Title
305.5'2

ISBN 1 84089 296 X

Printed in Hong Kong

Imagine you're a
Knight!

Lady Megavere

'The pen is mightier than the sword'
Meg lives in an urban castle surrounded by high
roofs and flint walls. At night when the drawbridge
is up and the portcullis is closed she feels safe and
warm and writes tales of daring adventures which
she will never experience (she hopes).

Lucy d'Ancealot

'per ardua ad astra'
Lucy, former damsel in distress, now spends
her days happily, in courtly splendour, with her knight
in shining armour, painting pictures
of her favourite things.

We would like to dedicate this book to our Knights in shining armour
Sir John, St. Jonothan, and *Lord Patrick of Holt*

What is a Knight?

Definition:

Someone who is awarded special honours
for bravery, chivalry and good deeds.

What do Knights Look Like?

A knight can have hair which is
brown, black, blonde or ginger.

A knight can have eyes which are
brown, hazel, green or blue.

Some knights are tall,
fair and confident.

BUT most knights
should have ....

gleaming white teeth

BIG strong
muscles

gauntlets

sword

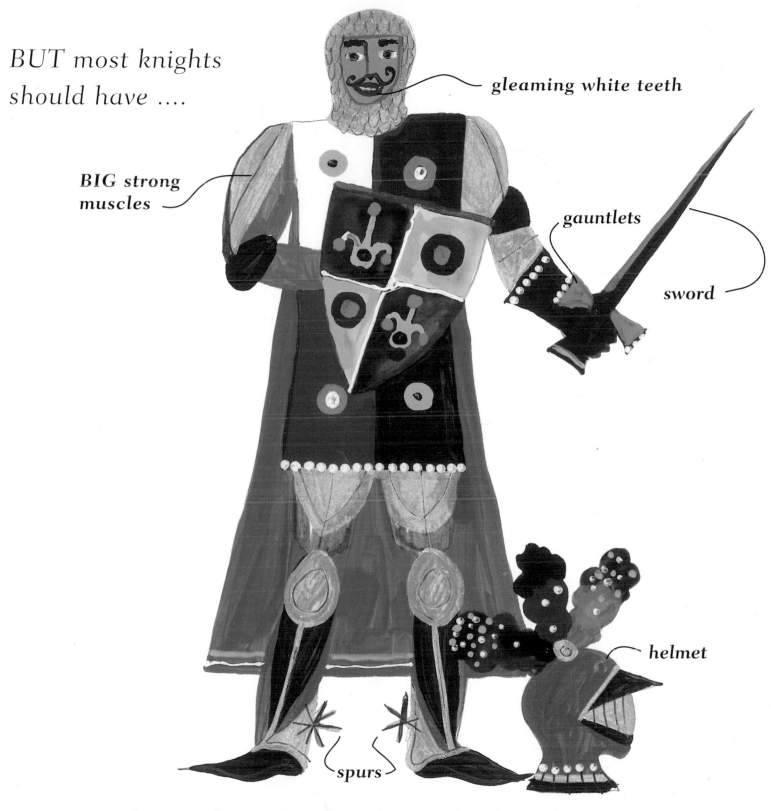

helmet

spurs

. . .and must be rather handsome (unless they happen
to be quite ordinary-looking – but very brave).

Knights in Shining Armour

The full panoply of battle armour was made up of many different sections. When fully dressed from head to toe, a knight could be wearing as many as twenty pieces of steel plate armour, as well as chain mail underneath, a plumed helmet, spurs, a sword, spear and shield. He was so heavy that a special sort of crane had to hoist him into the saddle and his great war horse would also be wearing armour. If he fell off, he was out of the battle because he could scarcely move. Knights of old were noble men who served their King with courage and faithfulness. They trained as soldiers but were gentle with children and women. They followed strict rules of behaviour and were excluded from the King's court if they misbehaved. They lived in castles from where they rode forth into battle.

and Damsels in Distress

In the days of medieval knights the world was a very dangerous place and it was believed that women (damsels) should be protected from danger. Girls were brought up to do sewing and singing and not much else. They were supposed to live safely at home in their castles but somehow they always seemed to be getting into trouble and needed to be rescued by knights in shining armour. Nowadays, of course, girls learn to do a lot more than sewing and singing. They appreciate courtesy and consideration but they can probably fight injustice and wrongdoing for themselves.

Becoming a Knight

If you want to become a knight you have to become the pupil of someone who is a knight already. You have to do exactly what he tells you for years and years and years. Not many people can manage this, which is why there are not many knights. You have to learn to be brave and bold and strong. You have to practise fighting (which is easy) and practise very polite behaviour (which is hard).

Chivalry

This is the very important code of honour which all knights follow:

1. Protect the weak
2. Fight wrong
3. Be loyal to friends
4. Seek justice
5. Be true, gentle, faithful and brave
6. Rescue damsels in distress

Dare to do right

Equipment and Accessories

Ladders for climbing towers

Swords, and bows and arrows

Chain mail

Carrots and sugar lumps
for horse

 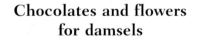

Chocolates and flowers
for damsels

Toothbrush (and teeth whitener)

Metal polish for armour

Helmet

Shields

Transportation

Knights have to do a lot of travelling.
They can either get out and about on a *horse* (very good for
adventures, and damsels in distress love them, but they need
a lot of grooming and looking after)
a *motorbike* (good for cities and built-up areas but quite noisy)
a *fast car* (the preferred option for long-distance travel
but not good for the environment)
or a *top-of-the-range bike* (good exercise and improves
muscle tone but only useful for short journeys).

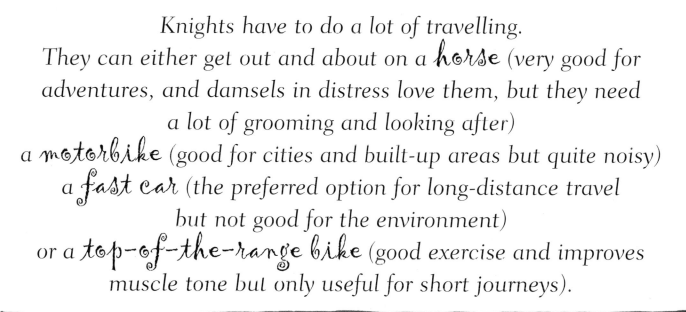

What do Knights Do?

Knights spend their time on quests, tasks and thrilling adventures rescuing people in trouble.

Quests

These are long and difficult journeys which knights make in order to find something. It is not always very clear what it is that they are supposed to be finding. It could be secret treasure, a firebird, a long-lost city, a famous sword or anything. Whatever it is, it is always hard to find and surrounded by hidden danger. The most well-known quest of all was to seek the mysterious Holy Grail, which was a special chalice lost in the mists of time.

Tasks

These are almost impossible jobs or tests which are set for knights by people who want to make life difficult for them, usually damsels in distress. An example of a task might be: find the secret drawer in the magic casket. Solve the riddle you will find there. Only then can you ask the damsel to marry you.

Adventures

There is nothing that knights enjoy more than going off with all their friends on dangerous and exciting adventures. They often encounter enemies and have to outwit them with cunning plans or fight them with skill and bravery. After these adventures they come home to the sound of trumpets and to waving flags and banners and swooning fans. They toss their armour to waiting servants and sit down to a banquet. What a life!

Rewards

When a knight in training has been on several quests,
passed all his tests and learned how to polish armour properly,
he is ready to be made into a proper knight.
At a magnificent ceremony at the palace or castle,
he kneels at the feet of his monarch and the
king or queen touches him on the shoulders
with a great sword. Then he is told, "Arise, Sir Laughalot".
He can then have his own coat of arms and motto.
A motto is a phrase which in just a few words
says what you think is important in life.

Modern Knights

Ordinary people sometimes overcome the 'dragons' of fear, ill health, disability and disadvantage. They sometimes do very brave things for other people. For this they can achieve the great honour of becoming knights. Oh, and you can also be made a knight for writing pop songs, kicking a football or helping to run the country.

A woman who has won the honour of a knighthood is called a Dame.

Dragons

There is always a downside to every job and for a knight there is a real risk of coming across a dragon. Dragons like eating knights, even the armour, so they are very, very dangerous. They live far away in mountain caves and breathe fire. Killing a dragon is not a popular pastime with knights. On the other hand, if a knight avoids being eaten by the dragon, he may win the hand of a beautiful maiden.

Kissing

When damsels in distress have been rescued, they often want a Kiss. Here are step-by-step instructions:

1. Approach damsel with big smile
2. Take damsel's hand gently but firmly
3. Pucker lips
4. Aim at damsel's hand
5. Make contact
6. Unpucker lips with smacking noise
7. Retreat
8. Keep smiling

Heraldry

When knights were all dressed up in armour it was difficult to tell who was who, and in a battle it is inconvenient to kill someone on your own side. So knights started wearing colours and badges to distinguish one from another. Pennants, shields and surcoats were emblazoned with an individual knight's colours and badge. These gradually became more complex, and coats of arms were recorded by heralds and later by the College of Arms.

Here are some of the symbols which are part of the language of heraldry:

Chevron   Cross   Roundels   Saltire   Lozenge   Bend Sinister

The Knights of the Round Table

Whenever we think of knights we always think of King Arthur who, with his adviser, the Wizard Merlin, gathered together all the finest lords of his kingdom and with his great sword Excalibur he knighted them. A hundred and fifty knights joined Arthur around the Round Table in Camelot and these brave and honourable men were sent out on missions to help the oppressed and to fight evil. The bravest knight of all was Lancelot, but even he was not good enough to find the elusive Holy Grail.

Things to do

Courtly language and behaviour

Amaze all your friends and family by practising some of the courtly language used by knights. Make up some of your own.

Design your own coat of arms

First, draw a shield and then draw inside it symbols of things you like or are good at e.g. a football, some crossed cricket bats, musical notes or anything that says something about you. You can then reproduce your coat of arms and use it to decorate your possessions or the door of your room.

Motto

Make up your own short motto.

Draw a dragon

A dragon is a brilliant thing to draw, with shining scales, pointed talons, a long prehensile tail and of course, fire and smoke gushing from its mouth. Make yours as fierce and menacing as possible.

Tournaments

Although kissing is very pleasant, many knights prefer fighting. If there are no dragons to slay or enemies to defeat, a tournament can be arranged. There is a sort of fighting Olympics which includes events such as a ball-and-chain contest, jousting, sword fighting, greasy pole, tilting and archery. This is so exhausting that the knights have to have a banquet afterwards, in silken pavilions, with sumptuous food and wine, and adoring crowds praising their skills. (Of course, it is very wrong to fight and you must never do it.)

Knights and Words

Silent letters

Have you noticed that there are silent letters in the word knight? Can you spot the silent letters in these words?

wrist fasten climb knife gnome
calf lamb wrap gnaw

Courtly language

Knights live in castles and palaces where everyone is very, very polite. They need to know courtly language.

Examples:

Your wish is my command, madam.

Ever your humble servant, sire.

Many apologies if I have offended you.

Please do me the great honour of allowing me to accompany you to the pavilion.

Eggscalibread

When knights return from quests and adventures
they love to eat this simple snack.

You will need:
a large lump of butter
slice of thick bread
1 egg
4 tablespoons milk
various toppings

Directions

Beat up the milk and egg.
Soak the bread in the mixture.
Heat the butter in a pan and fry the eggy bread on
both sides until brown.
Sprinkle with cinnamon and brown sugar, jam, or sugar
and lemon or trickle on maple syrup or other toppings of choice.
(Ask an adult to help when heating the pan.)